Shira

A Legacy of Courage

by
Sharon Grollman

Illustrations by
Edward Epstein

Doubleday
New York

For Shira and Ann Marie

A Kailyard/Laughing Bear Book

Contents

Note to Parents and Teachers

by
Rabbi Harold Kushner

One's first reaction to this book is likely to be that the story of the death of a young child is indescribably sad, especially when the child is as winsome, as lovable, and as vulnerable as Shira Putter. And we would be right. Her story is a sad one. Why then would anyone choose to read it, and why would anyone choose to share it with his or her own children? Because Shira's story is more than an account of incurable illness and inevitable death. It is a story of love and hope and courage. It is the story of a family drawn closer together, strengthened rather than shattered by the experience of illness and death.

Doesn't it frighten and dismay young children to learn that someone their own age can die, that their parents' love and their doctor's skill isn't enough to protect them? Yes, it does. But we can't shield our children from the fact that this happens. If they don't encounter it among friends and classmates, they will learn about it from the press and television news: the house fires and automobile accidents, the organ transplants that don't work. They will ask us questions about the children who die, trying perhaps to

VII

mask their own personal fears, and at times like that, we will be fortunate to have Shira's story to share with them.

Like Shira Putter's parents, I have sat at the bedside of a dying child whom I loved desperately and could not save. From that ordeal, I learned an important lesson. There is something that frightens children more than dying. They are afraid, if they become too much of a problem, they will lose their parents' love. They are afraid of becoming a burden to their families, making people sad instead of happy, until they force people to withdraw from them. Why invest all that extra caring, they say to themselves, in a child who has no future? If young people are frightened by the possibility of children dying, they should be heartened and comforted to see how Shira's family and friends surrounded her with love and comfort throughout their ordeal.

Children also fear that if they die at an early age, they will be forgotten. They will not have lived long enough to do anything memorable, and even the brief life they did live will have been so sad that their parents will try to forget it, to put it out of mind rather than be saddened by the memory of it. That is why I suspect they will be comforted to see the lengths Shira's family has gone to, to keep her memory alive. Illness robbed them of their daughter's body but could not affect their power to keep her memory alive.

Shira's poems and funny stories, Shira's hope and courage are too precious and too inspiring for them, or for any of us, to forget. The enduring message of this book is not that children sometimes get sick and die. We knew that before. It is that, in the word of the Biblical Song of Songs, "love is stronger than death." All of us, whatever our ages, need to be reminded of that.

Preface

S hira Putter died at the age of nine from a very rare form of diabetes. This book is about her life, her growing up, and her dying. The poems that you will read are poems that Shira wrote. The journal entries dated October 21, 1981, November 8, 1981, October 5, 1982, December 1, 1982, December 17, 1982, January 22, 1983, and January 23, 1983 were also written by Shira. The other entries, while not actually written by Shira, are based on what happened during her final years.

I first discovered Shira four years ago when my father, who writes about children and death, showed me a manuscript called "I Am Free, Pray for Me," compiled by Shira's mother, Ann Marie Putter. In it were articles about Shira, a short history of her life, and a collection of her writings. A note was attached from Ann Marie: "If any of this material appears to be the basis for a book, I would appreciate hearing from you."

That night, I read Shira's history. She was a small child at birth, weighing four pounds thirteen ounces. I learned the dates that she said her first words, took her first steps, dressed herself, recited her first poems. When she was five and a half, her parents were told she had diabetes. Her history suddenly changed. Instead of being a record of normal childhood events, the pages were filled with dates of Shira's repeated hospitalizations and medical complications. Within three and a half years, Shira spent over five hundred days in different hospitals across the country and had more than seventeen operations. The history ends with the details of Shira's final days—how she was allowed to die at home as she had wanted, in her own room surrounded by people who loved her.

Reading Shira's history that first time shocked me. I had never heard of anyone dying of diabetes. Didn't all the public service announcements on television say that the disease could be controlled by careful diet and insulin shots? I later learned that Shira was only one of a handful (less than 1 percent) to ever have had this form of the disease.

When I turned to Shira's writings, I was prepared to be depressed. I imagined her to be an unhappy child, dressed in pink Donald Duck hospital johnnies, forever lying in a hospital bed as doctors and nurses gave her one shot after another. But as I read Shira's journal, I realized I was wrong. Here was a smart, spunky, funny kid who lived her life to the fullest. Even hospitals became her home. She decorated her walls "that looked like peas when you squash them" with posters of rainbows, unicorns, and get-well cards. She starred in play productions in one hospital, went trick or treating in others. She always had favorite nurses and doctors to play games with and play tricks on. Hospital equipment became part of her life, and the IV pole she had to haul around for long periods of time became her companion Peter. She also wrote poetry. In her poems, Shira felt safe to express what was often difficult to say in any other way, that she was frightened and angry, that she knew that she would soon die. Shira was certainly a gifted and unique child. Yet, her poems and her life offer insight into how it feels for children to be hospitalized and for those children who may be dying.

I immediately felt connected to Shira, and I wanted others to know about this special child. But Shira's writings could not stand by themselves. Often there were gaps from one week to several months. Because many of the facts of Shira's life were not included, a reader could easily become confused and not fully understand her short life.

I kept thinking about Shira, wondering what she looked like, where she received her courage. I hoped that a book could be written that would not only recapture Shira's story, but her inner voice, the way she was. I wrote to Shira's parents about my writing a journal based on her life. Two weeks later they telephoned me, and our work began.

Over the course of the next year, Ann Marie talked her daughter's life into a tape recorder. My nights were spent listening to the tapes and writing down everything Ann Marie said—this was to be my working notebook. After listening to each tape, I sent back a list of questions, and another exchange began. I listened to more than twenty hours of tapes. With my notes in hand from Ann Marie, as well as a copy of Shira's writings, I started to write a journal I thought Shira might have written, using words that I thought Shira might have used.

Some changes are made in the journal such as the names of people, except for Shira and her family. Also, to avoid making the journal into a medical chronicle, the length of Shira's illness was shortened from three and a half to one and a half years. In no way is this meant to belittle Shira's medical difficulties. They were real and painful for both her and her family. But, I felt that they were neither the emphasis of Shira's life, nor should they be of the book.

While writing the book, people continually asked me, "Aren't you depressed all the time writing about a girl who died?" The answer was "no." Shira did not depress me. Her story was too much about life! When I did visit Redmond, Washington, Shira's friends, doctors, nurses, and family confirmed what I had felt and what I had written. One of her classmates said, "Shira was so special. She was the best of us." A doctor commented, "I see hundreds of patients in a year, and I've been in practice for decades. I remember only a few. Shira is one I'll never forget." Shira's grandfather recalled looking through his desk drawers after her death and finding little notes written and hidden by Shira, crayoned messages saying, "I love you."

Shira was loved. Her strength came from knowing that her family loved her and would always be by her side. Shira also gained courage from her religion. During the last year of Shira's life, she recited a special blessing every night, though it was traditionally reserved for only certain holidays. In this prayer, she thanked God for letting her witness and partake in this special occasion. For Shira, the special occasion was life.

This story is about a young girl's brave battle, her hope, her humor, and her spirit. This story is a celebration of Shira's life.

Acknowledgments

I wish to thank the people who were there to offer suggestions as well as support: Louisa Tarullo, Lea Wolf, Lex Wolf, Dennie Wolf, Pixie Apt, Betty Bardige, Sandra Bertman, Kenneth Sweder, Rabbi Kushner, Netta and Earl Grollman. I am also grateful to Wendy Barish from Doubleday for saying "yes"; to my husband, Thaniel, for reading every revision ever written these past four years and for believing in the book from the start; to Rebecca Davison, my agent, editor, friend; and to Mason Singer for designing a handsome book and Edward Epstein for his beautiful illustrations. Ann Marie, thank you for opening up your heart and for sharing your daughter's life with me. And most of all, thank you to Shira. May this book be an honor to your memory.

Shira's Diary

Prologue:
Remembering

Mom makes me sit down every day and write something in my journal. She says it can be about anything as long as it's at least six lines. I don't mind though. Writing stories is a whole lot better than math, and I like to write. Dr. Gupta asks me for signed copies of all my poems. He says that someday I am going to be the famous writer from Redmond, Washington. I'm not so sure about that. I have a very special kind of diabetes. Most people get better if they take shots of medicine, but that isn't working for me. Doctors keep trying to figure out ways to make my body work.

No one has said so, but I think I'm dying.

I couldn't think of anything to write today, so Mom gave me an idea. She told me to remember things about my life before I got diabetes and write them down. I thought about it for a while, but it was hard to remember NOT having diabetes! Mom looked sad when I told her that.

She said I should start where I remember. Before I went to bed she gave me an old picture that was taken right after we found out I had diabetes. In the picture I'm just like everybody else. I get up. I go to school. I play. I'm wearing my pink tutu and I'm smiling.

3

The Beginning

It all started last year. One day I was so thirsty I drank eight glasses of milk. When I drank two cartons with lunch, the teacher gave me a blue star, but later I wet my pants and cried. I was so ashamed, I wanted to crawl under my desk.

I slept at Grandma's that night, and I was still thirsty. Grandma was upset when I kept getting up at night to drink water and go to the bathroom, so she made Mom take me to the doctor. The doctor gave me a blood test and a urine test. Then she talked to Mom, and Mom called in Dad and Grandma and Grandpa. Everyone looked very unhappy. The doctor said I had diabetes.

We went to Children's Hospital in Seattle, and they told us all about diabetes. I had never even heard of it before, but I became an expert fast. A nurse told us that

5

having diabetes meant that my body couldn't take care of the blood sugar inside me. I couldn't understand why I had sugar in my body and why it had blood in it. When I asked the nurse about it, she explained that blood sugar is the name of a chemical that gives the body energy. Since my body had trouble using the chemical, I would have to take medicine called insulin to help my body work better. She said I couldn't eat food that had too much sugar in it like ice cream, candy, cupcakes, and cookies. I didn't really think about how much I'd miss eating them. But I do get jealous, especially when I see other kids eating them.

The nurse taught us about measuring how much blood sugar was in my urine and sometimes I pretended I was a scientist like Dad. First we put my urine and water in a test tube. Then we dropped a pill into it so it hissed and fizzled and bubbled like soda. Then the urine turned different colors. The color it turned showed us how much blood sugar was in my body and how much medicine I had to take.

Mom learned how to give me shots of insulin. At first they hurt. I tried to stay still and not cry. Every day I got a shot in a different place, so I wouldn't get too sore in one spot, sometimes in my arm, sometimes in my leg. Pretty soon I got used to them.

October 23, 1981

School was hard, not because of the work, but because of other things. As soon as I found out about my diabetes, I tried to tell some of the kids in my class. No one said much. Not even Jason and he was my best friend! Mrs. Katz, my teacher, told me she should be the one to tell everyone what's wrong with me. That day, when we were all sitting in a circle, she announced that I had diabetes. And then she explained what diabetes was using lots of big words, so I didn't even understand what she was talking about.

Mrs. Katz was mad when I needed to have a snack

6

every day during school to make my body work right. She said the other kids wouldn't understand, that they'd think, "Why can Shira eat if we can't? Why is she so special?" It was horrible. Mom said I had to eat everything at an exact time, but Mrs. Katz asked me to wait for regular snack time or at least eat a little faster. What was I supposed to do?

When Mom found out that Mrs. Katz didn't like me having my snacks, she and Dad met with her and the headmaster. Dad said that Mom really gave it to them. She gave them a huge lecture on diabetes and nutrition. It was funny thinking about Mom sitting my teacher and headmaster down and teaching them, but it didn't do too much good.

The next day Mrs. Katz gave everyone a cupcake because it was one of the kid's birthdays, and she let me have one, too, even though I wasn't supposed to eat anything with sugar. After that happened, I never went back to that school again.

In some ways I felt happy. School made me feel lonely. It almost made me feel worse than having diabetes did. At school I felt different.

October 26, 1981

Mom signed me up at the Jewish Day School. On my first day, my teacher, Miss Silver, explained to everyone about my diabetes. She said that everyone needs special care. Some people have allergies, so they need to have shots. Some people can't see, so they need glasses. Then she said some people have diabetes (like me), so they need to eat snacks and take medicine called insulin. She explained that diabetes never goes away. You can't get rid of it like you do a cough or a cold. You just try to make sure it doesn't get worse. Then she said that diabetes isn't contagious.

Every day Miss Silver reminded me whenever I was supposed to have my snack and then she let someone sit next to me while I ate. I liked it best when Joni was my snack partner. On my first day of school she came up to me and told me I was going to be her friend. Then she introduced me to everybody, saying that my disease wasn't catchy, and they better be nice to me. I couldn't believe it when she did that. I had known the kids at my other school for a long time. When I got diabetes, they all left me. Suddenly there was this girl I had just met taking me around and being my friend.

October 28, 1981

I loved it when Joni would sleep over. I wished that she was my sister. When I told her that one night she said having brothers and sisters wasn't too much fun. She should know. She has an older brother named Carl who loves to tease. Ever since he met me, he calls me Debra, even though he knows I HATE that name. "But that's your first name," he says when he knows very well that my middle name is Shira and that's what I want to be called. He doesn't listen, though. I can always tell when he's in a good mood because then he calls me Debra Shira, instead of plain old Debra.

It was great when Joni and I finally got back at him. Joni had slept over and in the morning, Mom made us green waffles for breakfast. Joni and I couldn't stop laughing. Mom shook her head and said we must really be tired if we found waffles made with green food coloring that funny. Anyway, we saved one of the waffles until it was really moldy and hard. Then we hid it inside Carl's pillowcase. Carl didn't find it until a week later when he had to change his sheets. Joni was in his room when he screamed, "Gross me out."

I wish I had been there.

October 29, 1981

Now here I am in the hospital again. It's the fourth time that I've been here in two months, and it isn't just for a blood test or even for overnight. It's for days. I'm glad

8

I have a private room, though. That way Mom can sleep in a cot next to my bed. She stays with me during the day, too, when I take tests to check my kidneys, my bladder, even my brain. But no matter what tests I take or what medicine they give me, my blood sugar keeps getting higher and higher, which means I have to take more and more insulin. When I first got diabetes I had to take one insulin shot a day. Then two. Now I get ten shots a day. Everyone says that if people with diabetes take their insulin and eat what they're supposed to, they'll be all right. How come I keep getting worse? I know something must be very wrong with me, and I wish someone would find out why I'm not getting better.

A few days ago they hooked me up to an IV. It's like a shot, but the needle is taped into the back of my hand. Mom said it looks like a pole on wheels with an arm sticking out of it. When I figured out how to walk around with it, I visited Dianne. She broke her leg skateboarding, and she was upset about being in the hospital away from her boyfriend. I told her jokes to make her feel better, but from the look on her face, I think she had heard them all before. I drew a picture on her cast of an elephant holding balloons in his trunk.

November 2, 1981

If I charged people admission to come into my room, I'd be rich. Yesterday I counted seventeen people. There were nurses, doctors, residents, dieticians, janitors, and people who work in the lab. One nurse made me really mad. She came in my room and asked my Mom how I was feeling. I told her she should ask me, not my mother. Then, before she could say anything else, I told her what she wanted to know. I said that my sugar went up to 600 today at 11:30 this morning, and it was the same at 2:00. She looked embarrassed when I said that. But I wanted her and everyone else to know that just because I'm a kid doesn't mean I'm dumb.

That night Mom and I both woke up at 2:00 in the

9

morning. It felt so special being together, just the two of
us, without any doctors or nurses coming in and out of
our room. I asked Mom if she'd keep me company. Even
though we were in the same room, I wanted to feel her
close to me. She crawled into my bed and she held me.
We didn't say anything at first. Then I asked her if I was
going to die. She said everyone dies sometime. I asked her
if I was going to die from what was happening to me now.
She said she didn't know, but she made me a promise that
no matter what, she would be with me always, that she
would never leave me. Then she said I'd be with her forever.

Dear God,

Please make me better.
Love,
Your old friend,
Shira Putter

Mom, I know I'm supposed to write six lines, but this is all I can write today.

Grandma and Grandpa visit me every day. I can always tell when they're coming down the hall. Grandpa clears his throat every other second like he is on a timer. Mom could use him to keep the beat when she plays the piano! And when Grandma walks, her shoes click. I like it when they come. When they're with me, I almost forget I'm in the hospital. We usually all stay together for a while until Grandma sends Mom and Dad to the cafeteria for a cup of tea. Grandma knows how tired Mom is, living at the hospital, always taking care of me. The only time Mom sees Dad now is during visiting hours. I know she must miss him.

Tonight Grandma and Grandpa brought me a deck of Snoopy cards. We played five games of Fish, and I won every one. Grandma pretended to be upset. She said that she must be getting old if a little kid keeps beating her. Grandpa told her I beat her because he taught me how to cheat. I guess he saw me peeking at the cards when I was dealing. We played another hand after I promised I wouldn't peek, and I won again. Grandma said I must have cheated, but I really didn't.

When we started another game, the bell rang in the hospital. That meant visiting hours were over and Mom and Dad came back upstairs. I wanted so much for Grandma and Grandpa and Daddy to stay.

11

I got up at 2:00 again. When I looked to see if Mom was asleep, I saw that her eyes were open. She got on my bed and we talked. I didn't want to get her upset, but I had to say it. I just feel that sometimes Daddy doesn't care about me. I know he comes to visit me practically every day, but once he comes he always seems so far away. It's like he can't wait to leave again.

Mom explained that Daddy does love me and that was part of the problem. He loves me so much that it hurts him to see me sick and in pain. She asked me to please try to understand.

Mom called Dad at the office and asked him to buy a stuffed animal before he came to the hospital. That night Dad came to visit with a beaver puppet who has big white teeth and a long tail. As soon as I saw him I named him Bucky. Mom was kind of mad at Dad. She said she asked for a stuffed animal, not a puppet, and who ever said anything about a beaver. She said that you're supposed to give sick kids bears, not beavers. But Dad was right.

Bucky's Bedtime

I have a Bucky Beaver.
He goes to bed with me.
I hug him and I squeeze him.
Because he's mine, you see.

Each day my Bucky Beaver
Gets up and plays a while.
He's a very clever Beaver
A friend with lots of style.

12

Whenever I go traveling
My Beaver comes along.
And if I should forget him,
He sings a ghastly song.

My Bucky goes to bed with me,
I like to feel him near.
Because he's very special
And so very, very dear.

I was so happy when the nurse came in my room today because she brought a card from Joni. It said

Dear Shira,

I am sorry you are in the hospital. All the kids at school give you a big hello. Last week our class put on a play about the pilgrims.

Get well soon.

Love,
Joni

P.S. Carl wants to write something so I'm giving the letter to him.

Dear Debra Shira,

This story is for you.

Once upon a time there was a green waffle who lived in a pillowcase. The waffle grew and grew until it didn't fit in the pillowcase anymore, or in the room, or even in the house. When the people saw the huge, ugly creature (they didn't know it was a waffle), they screamed and ran away, and the waffle lived happily ever after. He wasn't lonely because he made friends with the birds who loved to munch on his green, moldy crust.

The End.
Yours truly,
Carl

13

December 10, 1981

Mom and I are going home today! We're all packed and now all we have to do is check out and say goodbye to Dr. Gupta. He's the doctor who was so nice. I told him someday I wanted to be writer, and he said he wanted to be a writer, too, a mystery writer just like Arthur Conan Doyle. Sometimes Dr. Gupta practiced telling me scary stories about men wearing raincoats who chased murderers and kidnappers and killer bees. One day he thanked me for listening and said he was sorry that his stories weren't any better. I told him I always felt creepy after hearing them. That must mean he was doing a pretty good job, and he couldn't give up now. I showed him some of my poems, and said that someday I was going to be famous. I know he'll be excited to hear that I'm going home, but not half as excited as I am.

It feels so good to be in my very own room and to sleep in my very own bed. I wish I could go back to school, but the doctors say it's not such a good idea until my blood sugar drops a little. But they did say I could go for a visit. I was so excited! I hadn't seen any of the kids for so long. Hanukah is coming up so Mom and I bought all the kids woodworking kits or paint-by-number sets. As soon as I walked into the classroom, Joni and all the other kids rushed up to me. I gave them their presents, and they gave me a card that they made with all their pictures on it. Inside there was a poem:

> *Roses are red*
> *Violets are blue*
> *Come back to school*
> *Because we miss you.*
> *We miss your smiling face, Shira!*

We lit the candles and sang Hanukah songs.

By the lake God smiled at me
He made trees for me to see
Home again where there is cheer
You see, I really have nothing to fear.

15

Boston

Last week Mom, Dad, Bucky, and I flew to Boston so I could go to Joslin Diabetes Center where they know a lot about diabetes. Dad said we should do something fun before going to the hospital so we went to the Children's Museum and the Aquarium. But I was tired and sick and didn't have a very good time. Mom saw how I felt and said we should go to the hospital right away. When we got there, they sent us to a different building. There were lots of people, and it took a long time before anyone got to us. A lady finally called our name. She wanted to know if we had a blue hospital card and how we were going to pay for our stay. Dad filled out forms, and I lay down on Mom's lap. Then a man came up to us and said he was going to be my doctor. He told me his name was Dr. Stone, but if I wanted to, I could call him Uncle Richard. He took us to the Emergency Observation Ward. I wanted to ask him why I was so sick, but I was too tired to talk. Someone hooked me up to IV insulin, and in a little while I stopped

17

feeling so fuzzy. Uncle Richard talked to Mom and said he's never seen it happen before, but insulin shots just don't work for me. He'd try to think of something.

Our room is next to the nurses' station. There's a cot for Mom on one side of the room, a cot for Dad on the other side, and a hospital bed for me and Bucky in the middle. My bed is higher than Mom or Dad's, so I get to look down at them. Dad says our room looks like an army barracks.

Uncle Richard came in this morning. He said he was going to run a tiny tube called a catheter up my arm to a blood vessel. Then he would attach a pump to the catheter so that insulin would run right into the vessel. Mom looked excited, but Uncle Richard told us this had never been done to kids before.

To be in the hospital bothers me,
It makes me sad inside.
I'm really very frightened,
I think I'll run and hide.

To be in the hospital angers me,
That's where I always go.
Mom says this time is different,
That I shouldn't feel so low.

To be in the hospital excites me,
They're doing something new.
I know I shouldn't say this,
But I don't believe it's true.

To be in the hospital this time,
To get an insulin pump,
I hope they know what they're doing,
'Cause my heart's going all kerplunk!

18

My insulin pump will be special,
It will make my body work well.
Oh, if it really can help me,
Instead of life being so pell-mell.

I'd have a great time living,
And playing and running free.
No shots, no tests, no hassles,
Free to just be me.

Please, God, help the doctors
Make my pump work right.
Forever after your strength will have
made my world shiny bright.

January 22, 1982

Uncle Richard took me to a special room. He said I'd have to lie very still so he could put an IV in my arm. I told him I've had lots, so he didn't have to worry, I wasn't afraid. He showed me the catheter, and it looked like a piece of see-through spaghetti. But then he put the catheter in and that hurt SO much. I wanted to be brave and to lie still, but I couldn't. Uncle Richard told me it was okay to cry and I did. But I couldn't stop. Mom stayed in the room and held me until he could get the catheter in place. When it was over, Uncle Richard said he hoped I wasn't mad at him, and he was sorry he'd hurt me.

January 25, 1982

Since they put the catheter in, it doesn't hurt anymore. Sometimes, though, it makes it hard for me to bend my arm. Why couldn't they put the catheter in my little toe? I don't need my little toe for drawing or for getting dressed or for playing frisbee. Uncle Richard said he'd think about that one.

As soon as Mom found out my pump needed to hang from a set of suspenders, she went downtown and bought me six different pairs. The ones I like best have pictures with beavers all over them. Mary, one of the nurses, calls them my Bucky suspenders. She said that when she was a little girl she saw plenty of beavers, but never one as cute as Bucky.

I like Mary. At the beginning, I didn't think she liked me. She was so quiet. Every time I'd tell her about school or show her a letter I got from someone back home, she didn't say much. I figured she probably thought I was one of the kids who never stopped talking. But one night when Mary came in my room to check my pump, she handed me something. She said that it was for Bucky, but I could open it. Inside the box was a green and white jogging outfit! Mary helped me put it on Bucky, and he said thank you, then gave Mary's arm a big hug for both of us.

February 3, 1982

I got a letter from Joni today.

Dear Shira,

How are you? I am fine. When are you coming home? Here is a joke to make you feel better.

What has four wheels and flies? The answer is written backwards.

.kcurt egabrag A

Come home soon.

Love,
Joni

February 11, 1982

After Mary gave me a blood test, she got a worried look on her face. Then Mom and Dad and Uncle Richard came in my room. They looked worried, too, because my blood sugar was so high. Uncle Richard said they better take out my catheter and the pump fast. I felt too sick to care, even though I knew it was going to hurt. Uncle Richard said he wanted to try mixing a new drug with the insulin

20

I take. If it was okay with Mom and Dad, we'd start the next morning.

Before I started the drug, some nurses moved three big machines next to my bed. When I asked why we needed machines if I was just going to get a shot, Uncle Richard said it was just in case. Just in case of what? Did he think I was going to faint? Or maybe did he think I was going to die? When Uncle Richard finally gave me the shot, I wasn't so scared anymore. It was just hard waiting to see if it would work. We waited a long time. Not four to six hours the way Uncle Richard said, but for two whole days! Then it worked better than just plain insulin shots or the catheter and pump. And I am so, so happy. So are Mom and Dad and Bucky and Uncle Richard. Now whenever we get a good report about my blood sugar, we all start clapping and laughing. It's like finding out that we just won a soccer game, but even better than that. A trillion times better.

When Uncle Richard visits his patients, he lets me come with him. He calls me his chaperone. After he told me that chaperones were people who made sure young couples don't get into trouble, I said he had nothing to worry about. Most of the patients are older than Grandma and Grandpa. The patients are nice, especially Mrs. Greene. She's short and has gray hair that she piles up on top of her head. I like it when she tells me how she escaped from Russia when she was my age. She must have been so brave, but Mrs. Greene laughs when I tell her that. Every Thursday I help her wash out her dirty clothes in the sink and hang them up. She says she doesn't trust the hospital laundry to wash her rags.

I like Mr. Watkins, too. His room is across the hall from mine, and sometimes I think he listens to what we say.

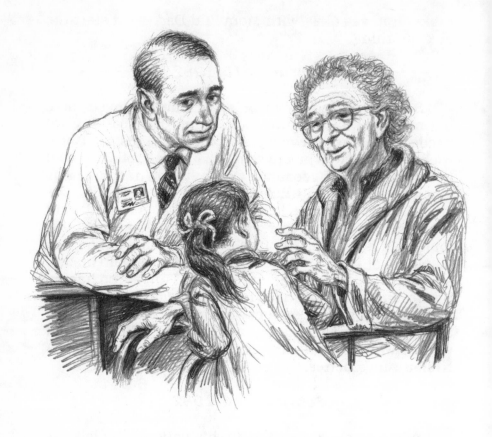

Before anyone knew about my pump, he came up to me and asked me when I was getting one. I asked him how he knew, but he just shrugged his shoulders. He must have heard us, which means his hearing is very good. But the other day I was talking to Mr. Watkins when a nurse came in. She asked him about his bowel movements. Mr. Watkins acted as if he didn't hear anything. The next time the nurse asked even louder if he had any bowel movements in the morning. Mr. Watkins finally looked up and asked the nurse if she said something. The nurse practically shouted the question in Mr. Watkin's ear before she got an answer. Mr. Watkins told the nurse that he had a very pleasant bowel movement during the early morning hours. I thought that was so funny.

Last night was special. For Shabbat, Dad bought a challah, candles, and some wine. Some of the people in the hospital are Jewish, so they came into our room, right when the sun was going down. Mom lit the candles and all the women helped to say the blessing. After that, everyone sang the blessings over the bread and the wine. Dad bent his head and said we should all say a silent prayer. I prayed that the drug I take would keep working and that everybody I loved would be happy.

I'm going home today. I can't wait to see Grandma and Grandpa and Joni. Last night there was a party for us in Mrs. Greene's room. A lot of the doctors, nurses, and patients came. They gave us so many presents that Mom said we would have to use two extra suitcases to get them all home. Bucky will now have lots of company with Amanda Alligator, Danny Dog, Mikey Monkey, Beatrice Bear, Louisa Lamb, and Regina Rabbit. But you don't have to worry, Bucky. You'll always be my favorite.

I never thought it would be hard to leave a hospital. But it is. Not that I don't want to go home. I do more than anything. But it hurts saying good-bye to all the people I got to like so much.

Grandma and Grandpa met us at the airport. When we saw each other, we just kept kissing and hugging. There was a huge sign hanging on our front door saying *Welcome Home.*

On Tuesday Mom took me to my new doctor. His name is Dr. Frank. Right away he reminded me of Uncle Richard. Maybe it was the way he sat me in his lap while he asked questions about my diabetes. For a minute I thought he was Uncle Richard's brother. Maybe they were

23

even twins, the kind that don't look alike. Maybe their mother didn't have enough money to take care of both of them so she had to choose one to give up for adoption. That would explain why they had different last names.

Dr. Frank looked over all my records. Then he gave me a check up and said the drug is still working. Yea!

March 11, 1982

I was really beginning to believe that I was going to be okay. And then my blood sugar got high. How come the drug had to stop working when I was doing so well? I was hoping so much that it would work because if that didn't, what would? How am I ever going to get better?

Mom and I are in Seattle now in Virginia Mason Hospital. There aren't any kids here, but everyone is really nice, especially Rachel and Karen. They're nurses. Yesterday they helped me figure out how to use my IV as a skateboard. Mom was with us, too. When I was skating down the halls. Dr. Frank stopped us. I thought he was going to say it wasn't a good idea to skate with my IV, but he didn't even notice. He told us there's a new kind of insulin pump in Toronto. It's different from the one I had before because it can run insulin into the body all the time, not just every few minutes. I can tell he wants me to go to Toronto. But I feel like we just got back from Boston. I don't feel ready to leave yet.

Toronto

When We Go Off Again

They said the last time,
They knew just the trick —
A pump's all you need
To fix you up quick!
Now off to Toronto, he says, and go fast!
They think they have something
Just the same as the last.
I'm tired of going to new places like this!
And trying to stay happy without friends that I miss.
Nothing's worked well and nothing's worked yet.
But you want me to smile and not be upset.
All right, I will smile and act nice for a while,
Even if I am hurting and have had my fill,
I trust you still, I trust you still.
But you and I know Toronto is it!
If that doesn't work
I think I'll just quit.

27

When someone asks me where I live, I feel like saying in the hospital. I'm never home! First it was Children's. Then Joslin. Then Virginia Mason. Now we're in Toronto to get a new kind of pump. Mom, Grandma, Grandpa, and I got here three days ago. Daddy couldn't come because he's missed so much work already. I don't like it here. The walls and ceiling are yucky green, the color of peas when you squash them. There isn't a telephone or bathroom in the room. If I need a nurse, I don't have any way to call her.

Mom promised she'd stay with me, but the hospital wasn't very happy about that. The first night we were here, Mom had an argument with the nurses. From my room I could hear her yelling, "My daughter is sick, and she needs me to be with her. If you don't bring me a cot, I'll sleep in a chair. I'll sleep on the floor if I have to. No matter what, I'm staying in her room." I was praying so hard that they'd let her stay. I need her like my body needs insulin. She couldn't go away.

When they finally brought her a cot, I thanked God for letting Mom stay with me.

I'm thinking about the Passover celebration we were supposed to have. One thing for sure, I wasn't supposed to be in the hospital. For the service we were supposed to go to Grandma's and Grandpa's the way we always do. I was going to wear my new blue jumper.

On the first day of Passover a doctor came in my room. He said he was going to operate on me the next day so he could put a catheter in my chest. Then the pump would be attached to the catheter. I wanted to ask him what would happen, but he was in a rush and left my room very fast. When I asked Mom what it would be like to get operated on, she said, "Sorry, honey. I don't know either." I felt so alone and scared. I wanted to yell at her to make me better, but then I looked at her and she seemed scared and alone, too. Oh, God, why is this happening to us?

Before the operation I had to get dressed in a special gown and cap. Then some men came in my room and put me on a stretcher. I held Bucky close to me. Mom walked next to me while the men pushed me to the elevator and then the men said Mom couldn't come any further. No parents were allowed near the operating room. Then the men noticed Bucky. They said they were sorry but stuffed animals weren't allowed either. When I handed Bucky to Mom she squeezed my hand, but I wish she hadn't. I had been trying so hard not to cry and now I couldn't stop. Mom started crying, too. I kept wishing that maybe, somehow, something would happen and I wouldn't have to go with these men. I wanted to get off the stretcher and tell Mom everything was okay. But the doors closed, and I was alone.

The men left me in a hallway on the second floor. Some nurses rolled me into a room with lots of bright lights. People wearing masks and gowns stood around me, and they were talking to each other. It was as if my feelings and thoughts were invisible to them. Someone put a mask on my face and said I would start to feel sleepy. He told me to breathe in deeply and count to a hundred. I breathed in the funny-smelling air, and the next thing I knew I was lying on a stretcher in a room all by myself. It looked like a tent was covering me. I thought something must have gone really wrong during the operation. I yelled and a nurse came in and told me that everything was fine. The tent was supposed to help me breathe. I felt sleepy and my throat was dry.

The next time I opened my eyes, Mom was sitting next to me saying that everything was okay, over and over again.

29

If someone even touched my chest where they operated, it killed. But the nurses had to SCRUB it. It hurt so
much! I squeezed Mom's hand and kept telling the nurses
to please hurry up or stop, but they just kept going. They
said there was a lot of dried up blood and they had to make
sure to get rid of every bit of it. After they were through
they showed me all the pieces of bloody gauze. There was
a lot. I asked them if I could save the gauze just so I could
remember, but they said it wasn't such a good idea. I'm
on an IV now and a bedpan. The doctor says if I feel better
tomorrow, I can walk around.

I feel a lot better today. The two best parts about it
are that I don't have to use the bedpan (I hate that thing.
It's so cold and uncomfortable to sit on.) and I can visit
the babies on the floor.

They are all so cute. Eric is four months old. He
doesn't have very much hair, but what's there is kind of
blond. He's here because he has trouble digesting food.
Every morning I visit him. Sometimes I tell him a story
or sing him a song. I love it when I can make him gurgle.
It sounds like a bird chirping.

Colin is ten months old. He's been in the hospital since
he was born. I feel sorry for him because his family lives
far away. They hardly ever get to see him. I wonder if he
feels sad all the time.

If I ever had a baby who had to be in the hospital, I
would never ever leave her. I would stay with her always.

Dad sent me the cutest card. On the cover was a pic-
ture of a beaver chomping on wood. Then inside it said,
"Wichewing You Get Better Soon." Mom didn't get it and
I had to explain that it said wiCHEWing instead of wish-

30

ing because beavers chew wood. A nurse gave me scotch tape so I could hang up Daddy's card over my bed.

May 3, 1982

Mom said I should write down what I do every day in the hospital.

—At 6:45 in the morning I get weighed.

—At 7:15 Mom gives me a blood test, and I tell her which finger she can poke that day.

—At 7:30 one of the nurses or doctors adjusts my insulin by turning the little screwdriver on the pump.

—At 7:45 I get breakfast. Every day I get the same meal: orange juice, Cheerios, bread, and cheese. The food here is pretty bad, but I'm supposed to eat everything.

—Between 8:00 and 9:00, I have to wait in my room to see Dr. Wiley. Sometimes I do homework or watch "The Flintstones" while I wait. I don't like waiting, but it's better than seeing the doctor. I wish he were nicer. Once I turned the TV louder when he came to see me, and Mom got mad. But he doesn't really talk to me, and he never seems to care about what I have to say. Everyday he checks my catheter and pump. Once in a while he takes me to a special room for tests and says that Mom can't come with me. I don't like that at all, and I let everyone know it. I might be very little but I can scream very, very loud.

—At 9:30 Mom gives me another blood test.

—At 10:00 I have school. A teacher named Miss Haskell comes to my room and we do reading or math. Math is hard, and I don't like it very much. We just started a new unit on addition and subtraction using money. But Canadian coins look different from what I keep in my piggy bank at home and it gets confusing. Reading is okay, especially when we get to read stories like *The Wizard of*

31

Oz and *Heidi*. During school, Mom usually goes to the cafeteria or for a walk. Before she goes I always ask her where she's going and when she'll be back. Mom says I'm beginning to sound like her mother.

—At 11:30 I get another blood test. Then Grandma or Grandpa and I do homework together.

—At 11:45 my insulin is adjusted.

—At noon I eat lunch. I get an egg, or macaroni and cheese, or a sandwich. For dessert I get a Rice Krispies square but it's not made with sugar or marshmallow. It looks much better than it tastes. Between 12:30 to 3:30 I rest and go to the playroom and do some homework. I also get a blood test.

—At 3:30 my insulin is adjusted, and I get a blood test.

—At 3:45 I get a snack. I like it when Sandy brings it to me. She works in the diet kitchen and she's really nice. Sometimes she'll cut my cheese into different shapes. Once I got cheese cut up like giraffes and hippos. Another time she made it look like different kinds of flowers. She brings me graham crackers, too.

—At 4:00 I watch the Carol Burnett show.

—At 4:45 my insulin is adjusted.

—At 5:00 dinner comes. Dinner is even more boring than breakfast and lunch. I get chicken and rice. Sometimes instead of rice I get part of a roll that's always dried out. And I get canned green beans that smell funny. It takes me a long time to finish everything.

—At 5:30 I get a blood test.

—7:30 is reading time. Some kids come in my room and Mom reads to us. Right now we're in the middle of *Charlotte's Web*. I hope Wilbur the pig doesn't get killed.

—Then I get another blood test.

—At 8:00 it's bedtime.

—Mom keeps giving me blood tests every two hours. I've learned to sleep through the tests and the watch alarm that Mom uses to wake up in the middle of the night.

—In the morning, Mom turns on the radio that she brought from home. Even though the music is playing, everything feels very quiet. Sometimes we talk about the nurses or doctors, sometimes about God and why this is happening.

May 27, 1982

Asha is my good friend here. She's from India, and she has Wilson's disease. That means her body has trouble getting rid of copper. Asha is always taking different medications, and she can't eat most foods. Except for some of the babies on the floor, Asha is the only one who's been here as long as I have.

Last week we put on the play *Cinderella*. I was Prince Charming. Asha was Cinderella. We got two teenagers on the floor to be stepsisters. Our teacher, Miss Haskell, played the stepmother.

It wasn't easy getting the costumes for the play. We had to go up and down the halls asking people if they had what we needed. Most of the time they didn't, so we had some inventing to do. I wore pajama bottoms that I tied in different places with green and red ribbons. Then I wore a long shirt I found in Mom's suitcase. I used a silk scarf as a belt and my fleecy bathrobe like a cape.

Asha and I made crowns to wear, but they kept falling over our eyes. I wore a sword, too, that I cut out of cardboard and painted gold. My sword was too long, and I kept tripping over it during the whole performance.

Mom said I looked like I was part of the royal family. She took some pictures of me so that Dad would get to see how I looked as a prince.

About twenty people were in the audience. All the teachers and kids from the hospital school were there. They laughed almost as hard as Asha and I did, and at the end we had to bow three times because they just kept clapping.

The new kids on the floor come to me and Asha for advice since we've been here longer than practically anyone else. Patty was just admitted because of problems with her stomach. Last night she asked me and Asha when she could take a shower. I tried to keep a straight face when I said that the only way to take a shower was by being in front of the shower door at quarter to six in the morning. Then Asha said you could only take a shower on Tuesday, Wednesday, and Saturday. Asha and I were proud of ourselves. The whole time we were talking, neither of us laughed once.

Patty wasn't very happy with us this morning. She came right to my room to say she got up extra early to take a shower, and the showers were locked till seven, and how could we have lied like that. I said I was sorry, and Asha did, too. We told her we were only joking. But I think she is still mad at us.

June 5, 1982

My pump keeps breaking, and no one ever seems to fix it for good. Dr. Wiley was really nice about it this morning. He said that since things have been pretty rough for me lately, I could go out on a pass today. I couldn't believe that Dr. Wiley was really saying this. It was the first time he paid attention to how I felt. I was so excited I almost hugged him. As soon as he checked my blood pressure and my hospital charts, Grandma, Grandpa, and I planned our whole afternoon. First we would go out to eat. Then we would go to the park.

All morning I waited for the afternoon to come, and finally it was here. I was putting on my red dress with the velvet belt when Dr. Wiley came back to my room to say he decided I shouldn't leave the hospital today because he wanted more tests done on me and the pump. How could he do that to me? Why did he have to wait so long to tell me? I wanted to cry so much, but I didn't want to

35

cry in front of him. And I felt like screaming at him for making me stay here when he promised I could go. I didn't say anything to him and right away he left my room without saying he was sorry. Then I started to cry. I wish Daddy was here.

Asha and I decided what we are going to do when we get out of this hospital. We are going to go to Canada's Wonderland. It's like a Disneyland with a big amusement park and a historic park, too. For one day we are going to eat whatever we want—no stale bread, no canned green beans, no fake Rice Krispie squares. All day long we are going to eat strawberry ice cream cones with sprinkles and fudge brownies. Asha won't have to take any medicines, and I won't have blood tests or pumps that have to be adjusted or IV poles to lug around. We'll be free.

Hi Shira,
Thanks for the picture. You look pretty funny dressed up like Prince Charming. Asha sounds nice.
I went to the Aquarium with Cindy last week. We saw a green moray which is a type of eel that likes to open and close his mouth. I'd hate to bump into him while I was swimming.
Here is a joke for you. What do Fonzie and a refrigerator have in common?
They're both cool. (Ha! Ha!)
Miss you.
                    Love,
                    Joni

Uncle Gerry is Daddy's brother, and he lives in Toronto. I had never met him before because he lives so far away from us. But now that I'm in Toronto, he visits me a lot. It's so funny because he and Daddy don't look alike at all. Dad is short and has light hair. Uncle Gerry is really tall and has dark hair. But they seem so much alike, the way their voices sound and the way they move their hands when they talk. They even laugh the same. When they first start laughing, you always think they're coughing.

Uncle Gerry doesn't have any kids. He's not even married. Mom says she knows a few people from home she could fix him up with. It would be so great if he'd fall in love with someone from Redmond. They could get married in our synagogue. I could be the flower girl and wear a long white lacy dress and pink flowers in my hair. Then Uncle Gerry could move closer to us and we could see him all the time.

Grandma is going home in a few days. Maybe she should tell one of Mom's divorced friends about Uncle Gerry and . . . .

⊢ *June 27, 1982* ⊢

Poem to Grandma When She Leaves Toronto

> Because you're here
> I always say
> You're the best Grandma
> in the USA.

> When you go home
> I'll always remember
> The times we had
> during this adventure.

> I'm glad you were here
> to hold me dear
> And give me love
> strength from above.

> When you are gone
> I'll think of you.

Please don't be blue
'cause you're you
        and
I'm yours through and through.

I'll see you soon
all healthy and new,
It won't be long
'till our dreams all come true.

Happy Birthday to me

Since Uncle Gerry can never find a parking space in the front of the hospital, Mom and I met him by the back door. As usual, Uncle Gerry was waiting for us. He opened the car door for us, and Mom and I quickly got in his car. I asked if I was being kidnapped. He said he was going to ask for a huge ransom for me and my pump. Maybe ten million dollars. And we better hurry before anyone sees the car pull away. I laughed so much because of the kidnap story. Also because it was my birthday, and it felt so great to leave the hospital and to feel free. When I asked him where he was taking me, he said he couldn't tell me because I might get in touch with the police or the FBI. Mom covered my eyes with her scarf. Then when she took it off, we were in front of my favorite Chinese restaurant. My birthday was perfect. Instead of a cake I got a giant fortune cookie that was bigger than Bucky. My fortune said that all my dreams would come true. Then a clown wearing bells and ribbons walked into the restaurant and headed straight for our table. He asked who Shira was. I could hardly say anything because I was giggling so hard. He said his name was Clancy Clown, and he was a present from Daddy. As soon as he started singing Happy Birthday to me, everyone else in the restaurant joined in. When we got back to the hospital, Mom let me call Dad and thank him for his great present.

We're on an airplane and we're going home! The pump still doesn't work that well. Before I left the hospital, the doctors had to attach all the different parts with rubber bands so nothing would come apart. I am really, really happy to be going home. But it was hard saying good-bye to Uncle Gerry. At the airport we just kept hugging each other. I felt sad, thinking that I might never see him again.

Home

Sometimes I wake up at night and think I'm still in Toronto. Then I see my dollhouse in the corner of my room and know I'm really home.

I saw Dr. Frank today. I gave him his present, a T-shirt that said "My friend went to Toronto and all I got was this lousy T-shirt." He laughed when he saw it and thanked me with a big squeeze. Then he looked over my hospital records from Toronto and gave me a check-up. He got a serious look on his face and told us that I'd have to be admitted to Virginia Mason right away to improve my pump and my catheter. Mom went crazy. She said we just spent three and a half months in a hospital in Toronto and now we'd have to be in another hospital?

I was upset that Mom was so upset. I told her I didn't mind going back. At least it was near home and Daddy could come every day to visit. So we go to the hospital tomorrow.

41

We're back in Virginia Mason on 9 East with Karen and Rachel, the best nurses ever. Four days ago I had to go to surgery so the doctors could take out my old catheter and put in a new one. But I wasn't so scared this time. They let Mom wait with me outside the operating room until it was my turn to go in. Bucky got to stay with me the whole time. Rachel even dressed him in a green surgical gown, just like mine. After the operation, Mom and Rachel were waiting for me in the recovery room. When we went back to 9 East, we found Karen's present, "Get Well" helium balloons floating all over my room.

Dr. Frank came in my room when Mom and Dad were there. He had a serious look on his face again. He said that he didn't think the small pump was safe enough for me anymore. So now the only way he'll let me go home is if I use an IV pole with a big pump and an IV bag mixed with insulin. He told us we'd have to plug in the pump most of the time because the batteries could run out. I had all these questions like how was I going to go to school or even get in and out of a car if I had to lug an IV everywhere. But Mom and Dad looked so upset, I didn't say anything.

Sometimes I think I must have done something really awful for God to have made me so sick.

Dr. Gold is a psychiatrist, and he's supposed to help me with my problems. When I first met him he took me into his office and sat next to me on the couch. He said I was going to see him once a week, and that during our time together, I could do whatever I wanted. I could talk or play or draw. It was up to me. And whatever I said was between him and me. He'd never tell anyone.

42

When I see him, I usually pretend I'm the doctor and the dolls are my patients. I always have to remind them to be good and not to move when I give them shots or hook them up to their IVs. Last time Dr. Gold asked how one of my patients was doing. I told him I thought she was tired and scared, but she had to sit still if she was going to get better. Then I gave her another shot of insulin.

── September 13, 1982 ──

I haven't been to a real school since last winter. I was a little nervous going back because no one had ever seen my IV and pump before, and I didn't want anyone looking at me funny the way they do in the supermarket. On the first day, we all had to introduce ourselves and say something we liked to do. When it was my turn I said I was Shira Putter and I liked to collect stickers, especially stickers with rainbows on them. Then my teacher, Miss Richman, pointed to my pump and pole and asked if I'd mind introducing my friend. So I said his name was Peter Pump, and he liked to give me insulin. Then Peter got measured and weighed with the rest of the kids. He's five feet one, the tallest one in the class!

── September 24, 1982 ──

Miss Richman is having each kid give an oral report that describes how to do something and how we feel about it. Joni is giving her report on raising tropical fish. Jonathan is going to talk about making robots. I'm going to do my report on how to take care of Peter Pump.

Most people's bodies make their own insulin. My body doesn't, so I need to take insulin. Shots of insulin don't work for me because I have a rare kind of diabetes, so I get my insulin from Peter Pump.

This is how Peter works.

First there's a bag of insulin. At the bottom of the bag there's a tube that is connected to the pump

43

which looks like a big square box. The pump pumps insulin into more tubes that are connected to my catheter in my chest. That way insulin will go right into my body all the time. My pump has to be plugged in most of the time in case the batteries run out. The pole holds the pump and the insulin since they are too heavy to carry around.

Taking care of Peter is something my mother does. Every day she gives me a new bag of insulin. Every other day she changes the tubing. By banging the tubes, she makes sure there are no air bubbles. Then she puts three different types of ointment around the catheter to make sure that it is very, very clean. When my mother does this, she wears a mask and gloves and I have to turn my head another way so I don't get any germs on anything. The ointments are cold and they sting. By the time my mother is through, it looks as if there's a huge mud puddle on my chest. Then she tapes gauze pads over the ointments so my chest looks like it has a mountain growing right in the middle of it. Finally, my mother hooks all the tubes together and turns the dial to say how much insulin I should get and at what rate.

September 29, 1982

When I walked into the doctor's waiting room, a boy came up to me and said, "My name is Tommy. What's yours?" Then he asked me how come I had to carry a pole around with me. Most people probably think the same thing when they see me with Peter, but they hardly ever ask. Especially two seconds after having met me!

I explained that I had diabetes, and I needed Peter Pump to give me insulin. As soon as I said that, he looked worried. He told me he had diabetes, too, and no one ever told him that someday he'd need to use a pump like Peter. I told him that my diabetes wasn't normal at all. Shots of insulin work for everyone else but me. I was the only kid in the world who needed to use Peter. Tommy said that was pretty special. I told him I'd feel special enough if I had normal diabetes. And my biggest wish is not to have diabetes at all. Tommy shook his head and said he had the exact same wish. Then he started in with his questions about Peter, wanting to know what's connected to what and why, what the batteries control, how the alarm is set off, what measures what, what drips where, how I walk with Peter, how I run with him. By the time Tommy was called into the doctor's office I was tired from answering so many questions. In a way, though, I was glad that he asked. It's better than people just staring, or when people ask me questions about everything but Peter, when I know that Peter is what they want to ask about.

Today was Joni's birthday party. Our whole class was there and it was so great! We all met at a rollerskating rink. Before Mom dropped me off, she gave me some quarters for the video games so I'd have something to do while everyone else rollerskated.

I don't know whose idea it was, maybe Joni's father, but someone said I should try rollerskating. I wasn't sure how I could do it with Peter Pump, but Joni's father said he'd help me and I said okay. I felt scared and excited after I put on the skates and Joni's father led me and Peter to the rink. Then we were doing it, skating around and around to the music. It was like flying. The other kids clapped their hands and skated around me. When Mom came back to the rink to give me a blood test, she was amazed to find me in the middle of the rink. She yelled that I should be careful. Then she yelled I should have fun. Even when I got out of the rink, I still felt like I was skating. I never wanted that feeling to go away.

I like rainbows and unicorns because they make me feel special inside. Even though unicorns are pretend, it

45

feels like there's a real unicorn inside each of us. You can make wishes on them and hope they'll come true. Sometimes at night I sing this song about them.

> Somewhere over the rainbow
>
> Lives a unicorn
>
> Flying pretty and free
>
> With his white horn
>
> Having tea on a star
>
> With a rainbow not too far.

October 8, 1982

I'm back in Virginia Mason. This time Peter Pump stopped working. I was so scared when it happened because if Peter dies, then I will, too. The doctors got him working again but . . . .

Dr. Gold came to visit me today. I told him I knew I wasn't supposed to feel sorry for myself, but sometimes I just can't help it. I'm tired of being sick and feeling like nothing will ever make me better. What do I have to be happy about? Every time I think I'm getting better, something bad happens and I'm in the hospital again. I feel like I am in prison and will never get out. The worst part is, I know I'm going to die, and it's so hard knowing that when I don't know what death means.

Dr. Gold asked me what I thought death means. I got mad and said I just told him a second ago that I don't know what it means. Wasn't he listening?

He asked me what I would want death to be like. I said I didn't want to have to worry about anything, about how high my blood sugar is or how much insulin I should get or whether or not I'll get an infection or if we can find a restaurant to plug Peter Pump into or about what would happen if the electricity went out and I couldn't get any insulin. Dr. Gold said he knew what I didn't want, but what did I want. I started crying and said I wanted to live!

I'm tired and scared and angry at God,
I want all this to end.
It seems like all my life
is spent waiting and hoping I'd mend.

God used to be my friend
but now I'm not too sure.
I really feel bad inside
because there is no cure.

I want to run away and hide
until I'm all better inside.
Maybe I could go away
and come back well another day.

Tomorrow Mrs. Richman is going to take some of the kids on a field trip to the hospital to visit ME! I am really happy and excited. First the kids are going to meet me in my room. Then we'll take a tour of the hospital. They'll get to meet Brian. Even though he's a new doctor, he's my favorite. He's going to take us to the Coronary Care Unit, the part of the hospital where people go for heart problems. Then we'll get to have lunch in the meeting room.

My class just took the bus back to school, but I still feel special because they were here. When we were in the Coronary Care Unit, Brian told us about the Doppler machine. He said it's kind of like a magnifying glass, but it magnifies sounds. Then he showed us what one looked like. The best part was when Brian asked us if anyone wanted to hear their heartbeat by using the Doppler. No one raised their hand, so I said I'd do it. I lay down on a table and Brian put a metal instrument on my chest. It

47

was cold and I yelled. That got Brian started. He pretended I was really a patient. He said I'd get better in no time, and I shouldn't worry about a thing. Then when the machine was beeping out my heartbeat, I pretended to cry. Everyone started laughing, and I cried even louder, moaning that I hurt and begged Brian to save me. Brian said he'd never let me die if it was the last thing he did. When I got off the Doppler to give someone else a turn everyone clapped.

After learning about the Doppler, we went to the pharmacy so the kids could see how my IV bags were

made up. When it was time for lunch, Dr. Gold came in the room and helped us sing the blessing over the bread. Was I surprised! I never thought Dr. Gold was Jewish. Knowing that he was made me feel closer to him, like we were related somehow.

After lunch, I said good-bye to everyone. The kids said they hoped I felt better and that I'd come back to school soon. Me too.

It's funny thinking that just a few hours ago everyone was in my room. Now it's just Mom and me. It feels quiet and makes me miss my friends even more.

October 19, 1982

When I'm in the hospital, Rachel and Karen give me baths. They are really careful because I'm in trouble if they get Peter wet. Tonight we sang "On Top of Spaghetti." Then I asked them where babies come from. They didn't say anything, just kind of looked at each other. I told them I knew it had something to do with men and women lying down, but I didn't understand why I didn't get pregnant because sometimes I lay down with my father or with Brian when we watch "Happy Days." Rachel said people had to be in love to have a baby. I said I loved my father and maybe even Brian, and Rachel scooted me out of the bath *fast*. I kept a straight face until I got back to my room.

Right away Mom asked me what was so funny. When I told her what happened, she said I already knew about the sperm fertilizing the egg. I said I knew that but I wanted to see if Rachel and Karen did, too.

I laughed so much I didn't scream once when Mom combed out my hair.

October 22, 1982

When Dr. Gold visited me today, he said he was going to teach me a trick. I asked him if he was going to make my diabetes disappear, but his face told me he wasn't

49

trying to be funny. He said he was going to take me on a trip and that I should sit down in a chair and close my eyes. He had me concentrate on different parts of my body. First I tightened each part. Then I took a deep breath and let go. After my body felt very loose, he told me to imagine a place I'd like to be and pretend I was there. I imagined the ocean and sand all around me. He asked me what the sand felt like when I dug my feet in, what the shells looked like, what sounds I heard. It was like I was really there, listening to the birds and smelling the ocean. Then he said it was time to come back, and I slowly opened my eyes. Dr. Gold said I could practice my trip trick during the week and that next time I saw him, we could do it again.

October 25, 1982

For Dr. Gold

My mind takes me running.
    I hear pretty music.
        I see myself running along
            the water and the beach.
            I feel so free.
                I leave everything behind me
                    and run as free as a bird with
                    no cares.

October 28, 1982

I wish I could go home for Halloween, but it doesn't look like I can. Rachel said I shouldn't be so sad because I could always go trick or treating up and down the halls. Still it's not the same.

Grandpa helped me decide who I should be. I told him I was tired of being a princess and everyone dresses up like witches or ghosts. This year I wanted to be something special. As soon as Grandpa mentioned Star Wars I knew who I'd be, R2D2. Grandpa said Peter Pump should be somebody too, so Peter, you'll be C3PO for the night.

Halloween was so great, even if I did have to be in the hospital. I was R2D2 and Peter Pump was C3PO, and we went trick or treating up and down the halls. A lot of the patients are really old here, and I think I surprised some of them when I walked into their rooms. Some gave me treats like pencils and erasers or sugarless gum. (I think Mom had something to do with that.) Some of them looked at me and Peter like we just walked off the moon.

The best part was the plan Rachel, Karen, and I came up with. We decided to INVENT a patient. First we found an empty room. Then we got a huge balloon and drew a face on it with black magic marker. Rachel made up a chart for our balloon man saying three of his fingers were cut off by accident at work. Karen found a rubber hand and let it float in a glass of cranberry juice next to the bed. It really looked like his hand was floating in blood. We stuffed hospital gowns under the sheets to look like a fat body. Rachel and Karen let me do the next part, hooking up two fake IVs to the balloon man. One had cranberry juice, the other grape juice inside. We were all laughing so hard I almost wet my pants.

Rachel put in orders for the night nurses to check the patient every three hours. I couldn't wait for a nurse to go in and find our man, and I tried so hard to stay awake. The head nurse asked Mom why I was so fidgety. Mom came to my rescue and said that I was just excited by Halloween and trick or treating. Then Mom said, "You know the ways kids get." I loved that! Well, the last time I looked at the clock it was almost two in the morning, and then I must have fallen asleep. But I didn't have to stay up after all because the nurse on duty yelled so loud when she found our man she woke me up. She woke everybody up. Even the security guards came to see what happened. I ran in to see, too. The fingers were still floating in the glass of cranberry juice and our man's head had shrunk and shriveled up like a sad old balloon. When I went back to my room I couldn't sleep because every time I started

51

thinking about that nurse standing there next to our fake patient I just burst out laughing again.

November 13, 1982

I'm home and just in time for Cindy's birthday party tomorrow. She's having a rollerskating party, just like Joni's. I can't wait. I'm going to wear the pink outfit Grandma bought me for my birthday. I feel pretty when I wear it.

I know that the first thing Cindy will say to me is, "How's Brian?" She fell for him when he put on his big act with the Doppler machine. The day after his performance, she called me up to say what a great time she had. She said Brian was funnier than Bill Cosby. I love Brian, too. Not in love, but I feel special when he comes to see me. One night I called him on his beeper, and he came up to my room. We sat on my bed and watched "Happy Days" together. After it was over he said he had a motorcycle like Fonzie's, and maybe someday he could take me for a ride on it. I asked him if Peter Pump could have a ride, too. Brian said he forgot that I had another man in my life. I asked him if he had a girlfriend. He said I sounded like his mother and then he imitated her in a high, squeaky voice, "So Brian, is there someone special yet?" When I asked him again if there was someone special he said, "Well, Shira Putter, you're pretty special." That's when I proposed to Brian and he accepted! We'll wait till I'm twenty and he's thirty-five. He said it's a long engagement, but I'm worth waiting for.

November 14, 1982

I just got home from Cindy's party. It started off okay. Cindy's mother said she'd help me with Peter Pump. We were skating to "I Want to Hold Your Hand" when something terrible happened! A boy bumped into me and my feet got all wobbly, and I was afraid I was going to fall. If I did my catheter could get pulled out. With all my

52

might, I concentrated on staying steady. Then the boy looked at Peter and me and said, "Why don't you stay at home where you belong?" He acted as if he was going to catch a horrible disease, and he kept wiping his hands on his pants. I was so mad and hurt. I wanted to scream, "Don't I have a right to live, too?"

Cindy's mother asked me if I was okay. I said I was, and we started skating again, but it wasn't the same. Tears kept rolling down my face, and every time I tried to wipe them off, they'd just come down faster. Then all of a sudden, my friends were skating in a circle around me. Cindy's mother said to me, "Shira, this is the circle of love."

November 21, 1982

Jane and Mom grew up together. They're really different though. Mom is so neat it kills me. Jane is the exact opposite. You can't walk into her house without stepping over things. But I love Jane. Since she moved back to Redmond, she feels more like a relative than a friend.

Jane took me out for breakfast today. Everyone in the restaurant kept staring at me and Peter—the lady behind the cash register, the people at the counter, the waitresses. Jane noticed it, too. She said I must be pretty special to get so much attention. I told Jane about the boy at the rollerskating rink and what he said to me. "That's special?" I asked her. Before she could answer I said I always *act* like I don't care when people look at me. But sometimes I get so tired of it. It's hard enough having diabetes and living with Peter. Why do people have to make it worse by treating me like I'm a creature from outer space who has no feelings?

December 1, 1982

Dear Class,

I'm in the part of the hospital where you saw me before. I came in to get my catheter fixed because it wasn't

53

working well. I was supposed to have an operation to get a new one, but the night before the operation I got very sick and my temperature was over 106 degrees. The doctors took a lot of my blood to see what was going on. They found out that my catheter got infected. Next my blood got infected, which made it so that my liver didn't work right anymore which is what's supposed to clean my blood in the first place. My blood cells are really strange now. I have had some interesting tests. Once I got a shot of radioactive medicine. Then I lay on a scanner and lit up like Wonder Woman.

I miss you all and wish I could see you, but right now I can't see anyone because I have to rest a lot. I can only go in the hall if I wear a mask because my body can't fight off germs.

Love,
Shira

December 8, 1982

Even though I'm in the hospital, Mom makes me do my math every day. I hate it! It takes me so long to do, and then when I do it, I hardly ever get the right answer. Word problems are the worst. Last week Grandma said that I should set up a lemonade stand because that way I would get more practice. Mom said she was crazy. I told her that selling lemonade would be a good way to learn my math. Just because I'm in the hospital doesn't mean I can't have any fun. Mom shrugged her shoulders and shook her head which meant I won. Then we started planning. Grandma was going to bring in pitchers, glasses, and lemonade. I could get water and ice from the kitchen. I would charge five cents for each glass of lemonade, three cents for a glass of water, two extra cents for ice, and two cents for an empty cup. At first, I thought it would be fun to have the lemonade stand on the Labor and Delivery floor so I could see all the babies. Mom said that no one might be having babies that day, so we decided to have it in the Intensive Care Unit. People are always in the waiting room since patients only get to have visitors for five minutes every hour. Karen helped me make signs to hang up on every floor. Then we found a table in the supply closet to put the lemonade on. I tied the Garfield balloons that Dr. Frank gave me all around the table. We used a bath basin to put the ice in, and we taped tongue depressors together to mix the lemonade with.

It was so great! In two hours, I made more than twelve dollars.

Then when we ran out of lemonade, I sold the most fun thing of all—kisses for ten cents a piece. When I gave Brian his kiss, he whispered that he was jealous that I was playing the field, and I should just remember that we were engaged, even if it was an informal engagement. I gave him an extra kiss and hug for free.

Karen, Mom, and Grandma helped me clean up when it was time to go back to my room and I counted my money. There was twenty-one dollars and thirteen cents! I figured out if I sold lemonade and kisses everyday for a week, I could make one-hundred-forty-seven dollars and ninety-one cents, which would mean I could buy hundreds of new stickers for my collection, a music box for Mom, a Mozart record for Dad, china love birds for Grandma and Grandpa, a Robert Redford poster for Karen, a joke book for Joni, a new jogging outfit for Bucky, and a ring for Brian. When I told Mom my idea, she told me to keep dreaming.

December 13, 1982

Today I went to the hospital for a check up. Dr. Frank said the reason I've been so sick is because my body can't take living on an IV system like Peter Pump, month after month after month. He said, because of Peter, my body wasn't able to fight off infections. Dad asked how we could stop using Peter if there was no other way for me to get insulin. Dr. Frank said that some doctors in New Mexico were working on an insulin pump that can be implanted in the stomach and if I go there . . . .

Dr. Frank saw that I was upset, and he came up and hugged me. I told him that nothing so far has worked. Why should it now? How many times can I try something new?

Mom just told me Dr. Frank isn't going to be my doctor anymore. I thought something horrible must have happened to him. But Mom said it wasn't that. He just thought I shouldn't be his patient anymore. I couldn't believe it! I loved Dr. Frank and I thought he loved me, so what did I do wrong? Mom explained that sometimes adults have a hard time dealing with children who are sick, especially when adults have a special relationship with those children. I said, "Yeah, and when those adults know that those children are dying. Well, I'm not dead yet." Then all of a sudden I got scared because if Dr. Frank could leave me, how do I know that the next doctor won't walk out, too? Then maybe Mom and Grandma and Rachel will someday come up to me and say, "Sorry, Shira. We can't deal with your illness anymore so you'll have to find someone else." Who will take care of me then?

Today Mom got very angry at me because I wasn't concentrating on my homework. She said if I didn't try harder she wasn't going to let me watch "Laverne and Shirley." I said I didn't care because I didn't want to watch TV anyway. Then Mom went to her room, leaving me in the family room with nothing to do but cry and feel bad. Mom came back five minutes later and told me I better get to work. I was so mad I screamed that I wished that she'd take a plane to Minneapolis and freeze to death. She said she wished she could burn up my math and spelling papers.

I went back to work and so did Mom.

56

I had a horrible dream that Mom said she was tired of me goofing off all the time, and she didn't want to be with me anymore. She was holding her car keys and standing by the door. I asked her to stay, but she wouldn't.

When Mom came in to give me my blood test, I woke up. I must have been crying in my sleep because my face was wet. I told Mom about my dream and said I was sorry for not doing things the way she wanted me to all the time. She was sorry about getting so angry and said that no matter what, she would never, ever leave me. Then we hugged each other and promised to try harder not to fight anymore.

Dr. Morrison is my new doctor. I can't talk to him the way I could with Dr. Frank. He uses such big words I can hardly ever understand him. The first time I met Dr. Morrison, he said, "A privilege to meet you, Sharon." I told him my name was Shira, not Sharon, but he didn't say anything. Instead, he told Mom that he talked to the doctors in New Mexico. If it was okay with us, we would leave for New Mexico in five days so that a new insulin pump would be sewn into my stomach. I asked how long we'd have to stay. He looked at Mom like I hadn't said anything and said "two weeks." I thought, yeah, sure. That's what they had said about Toronto, and we stayed there for three and a half months. Mom said we really didn't have any choice but to go, and Dr. Morrison said he "concurred with her decision." When we left the office, Dr. Morrison shook my hand and said, "Good-bye, Karen."

It's been too long
I've sung my song.
There's been doctors, nurses, an IV pump.

For two years whatever they've said
I've been made to skip or jump.

"They" is all the people who
treated me as if I were the whole zoo.
They poked, they watched, they wrote long words,
and even now, they're still not through.

All my life they've pointed to me.
I was too bright.
I was too small.
I wish they would go fly a kite.

I'm tired of all this,
of Peter too,
because no one anywhere
really knows what to do.

January 13, 1983

Dr. Morrison was right! We only had to stay in New Mexico for two weeks and the operation worked! Mom and Dad stayed in the hospital with me. Our room was like a hotel. There were paintings of cactus and horses on the walls, and we had our very own bathroom, air conditioner, and refrigerator.

Now I'm home with a new implant that the doctors call my second belly button. Today I went back to school without Peter. Joni ran up to me when she saw me getting out of the car. Then I told her I wanted to show her something. She watched as I got back into Mom's car, got out again, and slammed the door behind me. Joni looked at me as if I were crazy. So I explained that while I had Peter I could never get out of a car without someone taking Peter, then my books and my lunchbox, then me, very carefully, so the tubes didn't get tangled. Now I could get out of the car all by myself! I stood in the parking lot and screamed, "Good-bye Peter." Then Joni and I pretended that Peter was our true love who left us to go off to war. We pretended to cry and faint until a sixth grader walked by and started giving us strange looks.

Mom, Dad, and I went to California to celebrate my second bellybutton. On the third floor of our hotel there was a swimming pool, and I practically lived in it. It was great not having to worry about getting pushed in or getting splashed the way I did when I had Peter. When I first got in the pool I just kept laughing. Daddy dove in the water and pretended he was a shark out to get me. He grabbed my arms and chomped on my legs. When he got tired of being a hungry shark, he taught me how to do handstands and somersaults in the water. Mom said if I didn't get out of the water soon, I would turn into a dried up prune, but I didn't care.

The next day I rode a beautiful, brown pony named Samantha. The man at the stables said that Samantha took a liking to me, and he let me brush her and feed her.

January 20, 1983

Joni came over after school today. She brought her stickers and we traded. Since I like rainbows and unicorns, she gave me all of hers. I gave her all of my fish stickers. Joni said I was a rainbow and unicorn freak, and I called her a fish lover who should start her own aquarium.

Then we started talking about boys. I asked her if she likes anyone, and she said the boys in our class are pretty dumb. They are okay as friends, but she wouldn't want to kiss any of them. She asked me if I liked anybody. I told her Jesse is okay, but he likes me more than I like him. At school, he always wants to sit next to me or be my science partner. I just don't feel with him the way I do with Aaron, who is the most handsome boy in our school with his blond hair and blue eyes. A lot of girls like him, though, so he probably doesn't know I exist. After I said that, Joni admitted that she liked Aaron, too. So we spent the rest of the afternoon making up love letters to him.

January 22, 1983

Someday I hope I'll have a boyfriend. I want someone who is happy and smiles a lot. I really want him to care about me and love me for who I am, and be glad for what I do for others. I want him to treat me normally, to let me be free.

January 23, 1983

Ever since I read Judy Blume's book about Margaret and her bra and period, I've been really anxious for that time to start in my life. I'm excited, curious, and even a little scared about what it will be like. Last night Mom bought me my first lace bra. It has a blue bow and flowers on it. Mom says it's just a piece of material with straps, but I think it's really special. Even though I can only wear it for dress-up, I know that in my second drawer is my very own bra.

To me, being sexy means growing up but I don't really understand it.

January 28, 1983

Mom asked me where I wanted to go more than anyplace in the world. I didn't even have to think about that one. I told her I wanted to go to Hawaii. The pictures of it looked so beautiful with the ocean surrounded by white sand and palm trees.

All of a sudden, Mom got this funny look on her face, the same look she had when she planned a surprise birthday dinner for Dad. She kept smiling while trying not to smile.

"Oh, Mom," I yelled, hugging her.

Mom asked me why I was so excited. She said she only wanted to know where I wanted to go. She never said anything about really going there.

"But we're going to go, aren't we?" I asked her.

Mom said she wasn't going to say anything.

February 2, 1983

Mom needs to give me more and more insulin shots, sometimes seven a day, and I'm afraid to think about what's going to happen. If my second belly button stops working, then what? Oh, please, God, don't make me go back on Peter Pump again.

The Land of Parts

Imagine if you can
That our bodies are joined
With zippers and pins
And when we wish, we can travel
    to distant lands.

Instead of trees and grass
With swings and sand,
This land is filled with parts.

There's a table for long arms
And one for short,
A table for teeth and chins.

You get a shopping cart
And walk around and
Get what you need.

There's a cottage for blonde hair.
And one for brown.
And a shelf for smiles
And one for frowns.

If I could I would wander through
I would pick out hair, and eyes there, too.
I would choose new thighs and bony knees,
A long pretty neck would help finish me.
I'd add rosy cheeks and a dainty small nose,
All my fingers and all my toes!

Along the way I'd come to a room
I'd open the door with a sense of doom.

Here you hand the old used parts back
Especially those that don't work.
I'd leave off my pancreas and pick out a few
Zip it in and I'd be brand new!

On my last stop in the Land of Parts,
There'd be a supermarket of hearts.
Big ones, little ones, bad and good,
I'd choose a heart filled with love,
As I should.

February 9, 1983

I was supposed to see Dr. Gold, but I never even made it into his office. I was so thirsty, all I could do was stand in his bathroom drinking water from paper cups. Mom knocked on the door and said that Dr. Gold was ready to see me. He had been for five minutes, so why didn't I just finish what I was doing and come out. Maybe she was mad at me because she thought I was stalling, but I couldn't explain. When I didn't answer she came in and turned on the overhead light. But the light was too bright and it seemed to make the pain in my head get bigger and bigger. I held my hands over my ears as if I could hold back the hurt. Mom understood then. She held the cup of water to my lips and stroked my hair the way she did when I was little. Then I screamed from the pain. Dr. Gold ran into the bathroom with such a scared look on his face. It was the first time I had ever seen him like that. Mom asked him to please tell the hospital to make up a room for us. We were coming in.

February 11, 1983

There weren't any rooms for us at the hospital, so a nurse led us to one of the emergency room cubby holes. She smiled, saying maybe we'd like some privacy, and she pulled a curtain around my bed and the chair beside it where Mom was supposed to sit. Some lab people came in and took blood from me. Someone else put in an IV. And I just lay there, watching the dark shadows against the white curtain. I tried so hard to do what Dr. Gold had told me to do when I was hurting—to think about something outside of my body. I concentrated on listening to the voices that came from the shadows. If only I could have disappeared into those voices so I would not have to listen to the voice inside me telling me the second belly button wasn't working.

February 12, 1983

Dr. Morrison came in my room to tell us the results from all the tests. (Did he really have to look at the results to know what was going on?) He took out his appointment book, pointing to the date that I'd have surgery to take out the second belly button and put in a catheter so I could go back on Peter. Then he lowered his head and said he was sorry, that he wished things didn't have to work out this way.

Even if I didn't want to admit it, I knew the second belly button wouldn't work. Or if it did work, it wouldn't for long. Just like everything else. I am tired of being kept alive by machines, and I'm tired of them making me so sick.

Oh, God, why are you doing this to me? How could you let this be happening?

February 13, 1983

Mom got up in the middle of the night to give me a blood test. When she sat on my bed, I asked her very softly if maybe this time, I didn't have to go on Peter. "You know what that would mean, don't you?" she asked. "You'd die if you didn't go back on Peter, and we're not ready for that yet," she whispered. I told her I was ready, but she said there was one more thing we had to do—get to Hawaii. I said I didn't think I could make it that long. "You will," she said. She smiled, but her eyes looked so sad.

Dear God,
 Thinking about death makes me lonely because I know that no one I love will be with me. But life is getting very hard, and now I think I am more afraid of living than I am of dying. Please help me to be brave.
 Love,
 Shira

 Bucky and I were wheeled to the operating room. His stretcher was decorated like mine, with pink helium balloons and blue, shiny ribbons. Mom and Rachel each had a hand on one stretcher. On the elevator, a doctor who must have been new because I had never seen him before, said to me, "Great stretcher you have there. You're some

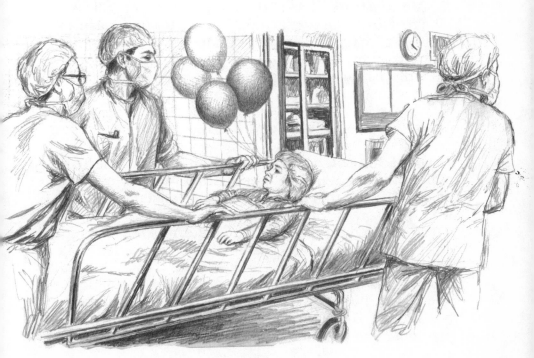

lucky girl." Mom answered, "You call living in operating rooms lucky?" Before I could yell at Mom, she touched his shoulder and said,"I didn't mean to snap. I'm sorry."

When we got to the surgical floor Mom had to leave because only hospital workers are allowed there. "I'll see you soon honey bun,"she said squeezing my hand as she turned away. Rachel stayed with me. While we waited, she took out some more balloons from her pocket and started blowing them up and tying them to my stretcher. But then I asked her if she could just stand close to me instead. Usually I can pretend I'm not scared before an operation, but this time I just couldn't. Rachel held my hand until an orderly wheeled me into the operating room. When it was time for me to get my anesthesia, Rachel picked me up and held me in her arms. The doctor put in the needle and everything became dark.

February 20, 1983

Mom cried so hard when she saw Peter. She said, "We're starting all over again. You're back on a leash, and that isn't living." I kept telling Mom it was okay. Then I started crying, too, because of Peter. Also because I love Mom more than anything, and it is so hard knowing that it is because of me that she's so unhappy.

February 24, 1983

Joni came to see me at the hospital today. She looked really pretty in a purple dress with a rainbow over each pocket. When I told her how nice she looked, she said, "I wore this for you."

We visited the babies on the maternity floor. We gave each baby a nickname—"Baldie," "The Screamer," "Red Cheek," "Monkey Face," and "Softie." Then Joni said that when she had a baby, he was going to have blue eyes and blonde hair, just like his daddy, whoever that would be. She asked me what I wanted my baby to look like. I just looked at her and said, "Don't you know, Joni? I'll never have babies. I'll never even make it to the eighth grade. I'm dying!" Joni leaned against the window we had been looking through and squinted her eyes. She talked to me like a mother giving a little kid a lecture about not looking both ways before crossing the street. She said, "You're not going to die, Shira. You've made it this far, and you'll keep making it." She turned away, and when she talked again, her voice was shaky. She said she had to get home to do her homework and ran down the corridor. I tried to catch up with her, but I couldn't so I just stood in the middle of the hallway with Peter and yelled, "Since when have you ever rushed home to do your homework?"

February 26, 1983

I thought I would be really excited to finally leave the hospital, but I was almost more scared than glad. I was in the hospital for so long and it almost felt like home. Dad would come every Friday night with his sleeping bag and overnight bag like he was going on a camping trip. But he had come to stay with Mom and me for the weekend. And the people at the hospital became my family. Karen and Rachel were my big sisters, and Brian was my big brother. I don't know what Dr. Morrison was. Maybe in between a father and grandfather.

Today I went back to school with Peter. I hadn't seen most of the kids for a long time. At the beginning it almost felt like we didn't know each other.

March 5, 1983

Mom tried to talk to me, but I didn't want to, so I sat on the couch with Bucky pretending to watch television. Dad took Bucky from my lap and put him on his hand and said in a low, sad voice, "Shira, I'm sorry you're unhappy." Then all of a sudden I started telling Bucky things I could hardly tell anyone. I told him that my disease is like a horrible monster that lives inside me making

67

me sicker and sicker. And now my disease was making me lose my friends. Everyone knew that Lori was having her sleep over party tonight and that she invited every girl in the class except me. I know I wouldn't have been able to sleep over, but I could have gone for a little while. I could give myself blood tests and adjust my insulin. I know better than anyone what I can and can't eat. Diabetes means my body doesn't work right, but I still need friends just like everyone else. Bucky said that Joni was my friend. I said I loved Joni, but we're different. I'm different from *all* the kids at school. Everyone talks about going swimming and skateboarding or going out for pizza and ice cream. What am I supposed to say? That my last blood test came out okay? That I hoped the next one wouldn't be any worse? That I hope I'll make it to the eighth grade? That I hope I'll know what it's like to get my period or kiss a boy for real? That I hope it doesn't hurt to die? That I'm scared that if there's no such thing as heaven, I'll never see Mom or Dad again. Dear Bucky, I hope dying is easier than what's happening to me now.

March 15, 1983

I had to go back to the hospital last week because I got an infection— a real bad one. No matter what medicine I took, nothing worked. I felt so awful that I didn't even care when Dr. Morrison said I wasn't allowed to leave my bed for days, and that anybody coming into my room had to wear a mask and gloves. It was the ice blankets that I hated. They were supposed to keep my fever down. But they were so cold, I could hardly feel my legs or my arms. Mom said that in the middle of the night I'd cry, "Take off the ice. I can't stand it anymore. Please take it off." I asked Mom what she did when I said that. She said, "I cried with you."

March 16, 1983

Dr. Gold visited me at the hospital. I didn't feel like

talking, so we played checkers. After we played four games, he asked me if I wanted to take a trip. I said okay, even though I was afraid that I wouldn't be able to see the sand or the ocean this time, only blackness because that's what I imagine when I think about death. At first, that's what I did see—a teeny room with black shades so no sun could come in and everything in the room was black. I wanted to open my eyes so I wouldn't see the blackness anymore, but Dr. Gold told me to take a deep breath and to stick with it. And then the light started coming in very slowly. Not just one color of light, but blues and greens and pinks. Then the ceiling and the walls started to disappear so that the room kept getting bigger and bigger. I wasn't scared the way I am at night when I dream that I'm falling. It was more like flying through a huge, open room. A rainbow land.

March 25, 1983

Grandpa and I had a big fight today. It all started when he said, "I love you, Shira." I felt sad inside because I love him so much, too. When I die I know it's going to be hard for him, and I don't want to leave him like that. I wanted to tell Grandpa not to miss me too much when I'm gone. But as soon as I started talking about it, Grandpa said, "Don't say that. You're not going to die." I got mad because I wanted to talk to him about how I felt, and he wouldn't let me. I said that I'll die without insulin, and the only way I can get it is through Peter. Even the doctors say I can't live on him forever. He makes my blood crazy, and I get one infection after another. What more do I have to hope for? Grandpa's face got red, and he said he never wanted to hear me talk like that again—that no matter what there's always hope. I told him I was tired and ready. He just walked out of my room and closed the door.

I was mad at Grandpa but I felt sorry, too. I love him so much, and I know I'm hurting him. Sometimes though I just wish he'd understand. I just wish he'd listen to me.

69

Even though I had a high fever and my blood was infected, Mom convinced Dr. Morrison to let me go home for Passover. Uncle Gerry flew in from Toronto to be with us. When I met him at the airport, he seemed surprised. I guess I looked pretty awful. I've gotten so skinny, my clothes don't fit me anymore. But I didn't care. I was just SO happy to see him, I jumped into his arms.

Later we went to Grandma and Grandpa's. In a way, it seemed like any other Passover. We said all the prayers. We sang all the songs. But when we were reciting the blessing, thanking God for letting us celebrate this special occasion, everyone started crying. Then, for about a minute, we all stood together quietly, holding hands. It was as if, without saying anything, I was telling everyone what was in my heart. That I loved them and wanted to be with them, but I couldn't make it much longer. That I wasn't afraid of dying anymore, so they had to let me go. They just had to.

I am on the shooting star
and going to a rainbow land.
It is warm and safe.

The day will come,
It does to some
When I shall die
And you cry.
After your tears remember
I will go to a sunlit land
With no Peter, no tubes, no doctors,
Just miles of ocean beaches
Where I will run
And feel sand in my toes.
I'll be free.
Pray for me.

70

Epilogue

by
Ann Marie Putter

Wh" hen Shira was five and a half years old, her doctor told us she had diabetes. It was almost a year later that she asked me if she was going to die. By that point, we knew that something was seriously wrong with her—she had been hospitalized four times within two months. When I heard her question, I looked away and thought, "Oh God! What do I say now?" I looked back at Shira with tears in my eyes, took a deep breath, and told her that we all die someday and that I would be with her always. Shira's question showed me that she was much more aware of the problems she faced than I was.

From this point on, I dedicated my life to trying to make Shira's life seem as normal as possible. I almost felt that if she did things that other kids did, there was the slight hope that she might be normal someday too. Even when we were in the hospital, I made sure that Shira was up every day, dressed and ready as if she were going to school. She had to do homework on a regular basis. She could not watch television more than she would if she were healthy and at home. I told her that she had no business feeling sorry for herself, other people had really serious problems too. Whether in the hospital or out, we tried to make ourselves feel that Shira was living a normal life. Even when she was attached to Peter, her IV pole and pump, she went everywhere, restaurants, movies, the opera. The doctors later said that this way of living is what helped keep her alive.

After we left the Toronto hospital, Shira was still hooked up to a pump. She spent the next two and a half years in and out of the hospital and underwent surgery many times. The catheters in her chest had to be removed every two to three months because the insulin clogged the inside of the tubing. Occasionally, the catheter would tear or become infected, and she would require surgery again. There were times her body simply didn't respond to insulin at all, and so we would rush back to the hospital, praying that the doctors would make the insulin work again. During these months, we spent many days and nights on the ninth floor of Virginia Mason hospital. Shira's "second belly button" was our last hope that she would be able to live an almost normal life. We wanted so much to keep her off Peter, to let her be free.

But the implant failed. Shira had to go back on Peter. For all of us, that seemed to be the beginning of the end. The few months she had been free of Peter Pump had reminded us vividly of what life could be like, something we had almost forgotten. Now she spent most of her days in the hospital. Her friends stopped calling. School became not something to work toward but a place that other kids went to. Death seemed more a reality than multiplication tables. The television started staying on for longer periods of time. She was physically and emotionally exhausted. Although Shira still wrote frequently in her journal, her entries were now about things that she would never experience, feeling sexy, wearing a bra, having a boyfriend.

As Shira became more depressed we looked for something she could look forward to. The idea of taking a trip to Hawaii was one we had to lift her spirits and to help her continue to fight. I still remember the look on her face when we got on the plane. She looked as if she were witnessing a miracle. But while we were in Hawaii her catheter failed, and Shira started to withdraw from the outside world and focus more on us.

When we arrived home, she went to the hospital for her final stay. I believe that it was then that she decided that we were ready for her to leave us. She no longer tried to fight the infections. She no longer wanted to have visitors or to leave her room. Unlike previous hospitalizations, she was not bubbly or joyous. She talked to only a few people. She was in constant pain.

One morning, after she had been in the hospital for two weeks with fevers, infections, and pain, she asked me to have the doctors take all the equipment away, she was too tired. I asked her if she knew what this meant and she said she did. She also said that she wanted to go home. It took several days to convince her doctors and the rest of the family that she should be released. Finally, on July 19, Shira left the hospital for the last time, looking quite frightened and alone with what she was facing. With her father and grandfather's help, she managed to walk into the house and down the hall to her bedroom. Once she got in her own bed, she smiled a beautiful smile of a-chievement. She knew she had come home to die, surrounded by people who loved her.

Shira slept deeply, as if preparing herself to leave us. I sat by her bed and took her hands. I told her how special she had always been and that I hoped that she would find her rainbow and her unicorns. I cried as I sang to her. Only July 26, I knelt down next to her bed. She took a little breath and relaxed. Then nothing. "No," I screamed. Then I looked at her face and cried, "You're free now, doll. It's okay, you're free."

Under traditional Jewish law a funeral must take place within twenty-four hours after a person dies, so the following day Shira was buried. Following the service at the cemetery I looked back as we drove and was shocked to seen an endless row of cars following us. There were

75

so many I couldn't see the end. So many people loved Shira and were coming to show that love.

The next seven days of mourning were followed according to our traditional laws with daily religious services except on the Sabbath. During that week, several hundred people came to our house to share our grief with us. I found our traditional laws comforting as they gave an order to my days.

Finally, those seven days ended, and although I attended services daily, people weren't always around me. I felt lost. For years my whole life had been caring for Shira, watching what she ate, taking care of her insulin, her pumps. It was a twenty-four hour job. Now there was nothing. My relief that Shira was not in pain turned into shock that she had actually died. I now felt a different kind of pain, the pain of never again hearing her voice, the pain of not seeing her grow up. There would never be another dress to buy, another ballet to go to together. I mourned for all the might-have-beens. The deep grief I had for Shira was just as great as my love. My grief made it difficult to think of or talk about anyone but Shira. Life felt empty. The future felt overwhelming.

One good thing that helped us deal with our grief was recognizing that as two people, Shira's father and I were grieving in different ways. He seldom cried at home—but did in the privacy of his office or car. I cried at home and with my parents, Shira's grandparents. He was patient when I needed comforting, and I tried to understand when he was silent. We both were hurting, but we dealt with Shira's death differently. This understanding of each other's needs has made us very close.

In time, the overwhelming grief has begun to be replaced by the feeling of wonder that Shira had been— and still is—such a blessing in our lives. She brings us such joy. We knew that she didn't want to live as she had been living—not able to go to school or do anything, with only the possibility of getting worse. As she got older, her medical complications would have increased, and her social isolation would have been more difficult. So it became easier to let go of the pain of "if only she had lived."

Instead we have begun to focus on the joy and excitement she brought to us when she was young and her courage and strength while she was ill. We thought of the happiness she brought to all the people who knew her— her inherent goodness and love of people.

It is almost five years since Shira died. Although I miss her and always will, the pain and grief are much easier to deal with. I no longer look at Bucky Beaver and cry—I just feel sad because he seems lonely. I think of Shira often. It is not with pain but with joy that she spent time with us. I now marvel at all we did during her short life.

I still hurt, of course. Her birthday, special holidays, particularly Passover, are difficult times. But Shira's life and death have made me grow in ways I never would have. Because of Shira, I am more aware of people's pain, more compassionate and caring. I know more about myself and about people and friendships. My view of the grass and sun is different than someone who has not lost a person they love. I am a better human being because of Shira. Her strength and love have made me stronger and more loving. I have come through this okay—I have grown. My vision of tomorrow is colored by my yesterday, and I would not be who I am today if Shira were not a part of me.

Recommended Resources

Organizations

Compassionate Friends
Post Office Box 1347
Oak Brook, Illinois 60521
This is the group that helped Shira's mother during her grief. It is an international organization made up of parents who have lost a child.

Forum for Death Education and Counseling
2211 Arthur Avenue
Lakewood, Ohio 44107
This organization disseminates information about death education and counseling.

Hospice

The hospice movement helps not only the dying patient but supports the family as a unit. For more information, contact:

National Institute for Jewish Hospice
6363 Wilshire Blvd.
Los Angeles, CA 90048

National Hospice Organization
1901 North Fort Myer Drive, Suite 307
Arlington, VA 22209

Children's Hospice International
1101 King Street, Suite 131
Alexandria, VA 22314

Books

For Children

Judy Blume, **Tiger Eyes.** Scarsdale, New York: Bradbury Press, 1981. *Ages 11 and up. A novel about a young girl and how she deals with her father's murder.*

Leo Buscaglia, **The Fall of Freddie the Leaf.** New York: Holt, Rinehart, and Winston, 1982. *Preschool and up. An allegorical story about how Freddie, the leaf, changes with the seasons. In the end, Freddie and his leaf companions, fall to the ground with the white snow.*

Center for Attitudinal Healing, **There is a Rainbow behind Every Dark Cloud.** Berkeley, CA: Celestial Arts, 1979. *Ages 5 to 12. Through pictures and words, children talk about how they come to terms with their terminal illness.*

Eleanor Coerr, **Sadako and the Thousand Paper Cranes.** New York: Putnam, 1977. *Ages 12 to 14. The true story of a young girl, Sadako, who died as a result of leukemia caused by the atomic bombing of Hiroshima. The book describes the last year of Sadako's life.*

Constance C. Greene, **Beat the Turtle Drum.** New York: Viking, 1976. *Ages 9 to 13. A realistic and sensitive story about Joss and her older sister, Kate. Both love horses and save enough money to rent a horse for a week. It is a happy time for the sisters until Joss falls from a tree, dying instantly.*

Earl A. Grollman, **Talking about Death: A Dialogue between Parent and Child.** Boston: Beacon Press, 1976. *Preschool and up. The author, a Rabbi and leading authority in the field of death education, discusses death in an honest, sensitive, straightforward matter. The book also includes a parents' guide and an annotated list of resources.*

Eda LeShan, **Learning to Say Good-by: When a Parent Dies.** New York: Macmillan, 1978. *Ages 10 and up. This informative and supportive book, written by a family counselor, addresses problems children face when they lose a parent, and how these problems may be overcome.*

Miska Miles, **Annie and the Old One.** Boston: Little Brown and Co., 1971. *Ages 8 to 12. A beautiful story about an Indian girl who tries to postpone her grandmother's death. The Old One teaches her granddaughter that the order of nature cannot be changed.*

Katherine Patterson, **Bridge to Terabithia.** New York: Crowell, 1977. *Ages 9 to 12. Two children, Jess and Leslie, create Terabithia, a secret kingdom in the woods. Tragedy occurs when Leslie is killed in an accident on her way to Terabithia.*

Elizabeth Richter, **Losing Someone You Love.** New York: Putnam, 1986. *Ages 10 and up. Young people discuss their experiences when a sibling dies.*

Eric E. Rofes, and The Unit at Fayerweather Street School, **The Kids' Book about Death and Dying.** Boston: Little Brown and Co., 1985. *Ages 11 and up. Children between ages of 11 and 14 write about their experiences with death, their fears, and their fantasies.*

Alfred Slote, **Hang Tough, Paul Mather.** Philadelphia: Lippincott, 1973. *Ages 8 to 12. A moving sports story about a twelve-year-old boy and his battle against leukemia and his baseball opponents.*

Doris B. Smith, **A Taste of Blackberries.** New York: Crowell, 1973. *Ages 8 to 12. In this Child Study Association Award-winning book, a boy struggles with his grief when his best friend dies as a result of an allergic reaction to bee stings.*

Sara Bonnett Stein, **About Dying.** New York: Walker, 1974. *Preschool to 9. Two narratives are included in this book. One is for parents. It explains children's conceptions and possible reactions to death. The other narrative is for children. It depicts one youngster's responses to the death of a pet and a grandfather.*

Judith Viorst, **The Tenth Good Thing about Barney.** New York: Atheneum, 1971. *Ages 5 to 9. When Barney the cat dies, his young owner tries to think of ten good things to say at the funeral. He can only think of nine. Then, while working in the garden, the boy discovers the tenth good thing, Barney will now help things grow.*

E.B. White, **Charlotte's Web.** New York: Harper and Row, 1952. *Ages 8 to 11. When Charlotte, the spider, dies at the fairgrounds, her animal friends manage to take her eggs back to the farm where they can safely hatch. A classic story that portrays the beauty and significance of friendship.*

For Adults

Myra Bluebond-Langner, **The Private Worlds of Dying Children.** Princeton, New Jersey: Princeton University Press, 1978. *An anthropologist's insightful descriptions of children with leukemia whom she observed in a hospital pediatric ward.*

Elisabeth Kubler-Ross, **On Children and Death.** New York: Macmillan, 1983. *Offers practical and loving help to parents of dying children.*

Harold Kushner, **When Bad Things Happen to Good People.** New York: Schocken, 1981. *This acclaimed national bestseller has brought comfort to millions who have suffered a loss.*

Richard Lonetto, **Children's Conceptions of Death.** New York: Springer, 1980. *Presents a development picture of children's understanding of death between the ages of 3 and 12.*

Hannelore Wass and Charles A. Corr, (eds.) **Helping Children Cope with Death: Guidelines and Resources,** (2d ed.) Washington, D.C.: Hemisphere, 1984. *Gives practical guidelines for death education and a comprehensive listing of resources.*

Glossary/Index

Anesthesia, 65. *During an operation, a chemical is given that stops the feeling of pain. General anesthesia numbs the patient's entire body, which causes a kind of sleep. The patient does not wake up until the operation is completed.*

Blood sugar, 6, 9, 15, 20, 21, 24, 46. *A chemical that gives the body energy. When the blood sugar is too high or too low, a person can feel tired, weak, shaky, and dizzy.*

Blood test, 5, 8, 20, 31, 32, 45, 64, 67. *Blood is taken by pricking the finger. By studying the blood sample, doctors and nurses can tell whether a person is healthy or if an infection is present. Shira needed blood tests to determine how high her blood sugar was, and how much insulin she needed to take.*

Blood vessel, 18. *The parts of the body that carry blood to and from the heart.*

Catheter, 18, 19, 20, 21, 28, 31, 41, 42, 44, 52, 53, 54, 74. *A tiny plastic tube that is inserted into the body, usually the vein. Medicine or liquid food can then be injected into the body through the catheter.*

Challah, 23. *Bread that is eaten on the Jewish Sabbath.*

Coronary Care Unit, 47. *A part of the hospital for people with heart problems.*

Diabetes, 3, 5, 6, 7, 8, 23, 44, 45, 49, 53, 67. *A disease in which the body cannot use sugar properly. It is not contagious, and it can normally be controlled with a careful diet and insulin shots.*

Dietician, 9. *A person in the hospital who decides what patients should eat.*

Doppler machine, 47, 48, 52. *A machine that uses sound to measure the flow of blood.*

82

Hanukah, 15. *An eight-day Jewish holiday that celebrates the victory of the Jewish soldiers and the rededication of the Temple in Jerusalem in 165 B.C.E. On each night of this holiday, candles are lit and gifts are exchanged.*

Insulin, 7, 18, 21, 25, 31, 32, 43, 44, 46, 55, 57, 61, 67, 69. *A special chemical that the body needs to get energy from sugar. When people have diabetes, either their bodies cannot make enough insulin, or the insulin does not work the way it should. Insulin shots are then needed so that their bodies can function properly.*

Intensive Care Unit, 54. *The part of the hospital where seriously ill people are cared for.*

IV, 9, 17, 25, 42, 43, 48, 51, 55, 57, 74. *An abbreviation for "intravenous." When someone is hooked up to an IV, a needle is taped into the back of the hand. The needle is then attached to tubes that lead to a bottle of medicine or liquid food that hangs from a big pole. The liquid drips into a tube, then travels through the needle into the vein.*

Maternity floor, 66. *The part of the hospital where mothers stay with their new babies.*

Passover, 28, 70, 77. *This eight-day Jewish holiday cel-ebrates the escape of the Jews from ancient Egypt. On the first two nights of Passover, family and friends gather together to retell the story of the escape and partake in a traditional meal.*

"Peter" Pump, 18, 19, 20, 21, 27, 28, 39, 41, 42, 43, 44, 46, 57, 74. *For long periods of time, Shira used an IV pole with a big pump that she called Peter. Peter constantly pumped insulin into Shira's catheter, which was inserted in a large vein in Shira's chest.*

Psychiatrist, 42. *A doctor who helps people with their emotional problems.*

Scanner (gamma), 54. *Liquid is injected into the patient's vein. The scanner traces the liquid as it flows through the body.*

Shabbat, 23. *The Jewish Sabbath begins Friday at sundown and ends Saturday at sunset. On this day of rest, blessings are said over the candles, wine, and bread.*

Synagogue, 37. *A Jewish house of worship.*

Urine test, 5. *A pill is dropped into a sample of urine. The color the urine turns shows how much sugar is in the body and how much insulin needs to be taken.*

The illustrator of this volume dedicates his work to the memory of his wife.

Myra Wasserman Epstein
November 25, 1942 - February 19, 1985

Like Shira, Molly's all too short life was circumscribed by a long struggle with the difficulties of diabetes. As a highly praised artist and designer, Molly, too, shares a permanent place in the memories of all who knew her.

84